Original title:
The Echo of Leaves

Copyright © 2025 Creative Arts Management OÜ
All rights reserved.

Author: Zachary Prescott
ISBN HARDBACK: 978-1-80581-896-0
ISBN PAPERBACK: 978-1-80581-423-8
ISBN EBOOK: 978-1-80581-896-0

Echoes of Earthly Beauty

In the park, they dance and twirl,
High above, the branches whirl.
Squirrels chatter, what a sight,
Acorns falling left and right.

Frogs are croaking, quite the cheer,
While a bee flies in my ear.
Nature's comedy unfolds,
With secrets waiting to be told.

Resonant Passages of Nature

Rustling whispers through the trees,
Playful antics in the breeze.
A chipmunk counts its stash of nuts,
While a crow laughs at someone's guts.

Leaves plan parties, bark is their cape,
In this wild and leafy landscape.
Who knew they were such good friends?
Nature's laughter never ends.

Leaves That Speak in Silence

Underfoot, a crunch is heard,
Is it gossip, or just a bird?
Winds gossip, swirling round,
With secrets that astound the ground.

Bending low, the branches tease,
Swinging gently with such ease.
Nature shrugs, with an unseen grin,
At all the silliness within.

Harmonies of Past and Present

Old roots chuckle from below,
As seeds of laughter start to grow.
The sunbeams wink, a quirky jest,
While shadows hide and never rest.

Together they hum a sweet old tune,
Both night and day, sun and moon.
Leaves stretch wide on a carefree day,
Who knew nature liked to play?

Whispers in the Canopy

In the treetops, whispers fly,
Squirrels giggle, oh me, oh my!
Branches sway, a dance in place,
Leaves throw shade, what's this embrace?

A woodpecker knocks with flair,
Says, "Who's there?" to the air.
The breeze joins in with a chuckle,
Nature's jest, a lively knuckle!

Rustling Memories

Once a leaf had quite a tale,
Of a snail who stole a rail.
He left a trail of sticky slime,
Nature's prank, it is prime time!

Through the wind, old laughter roams,
As critters share their leafy homes.
They sit in circles, swap their lore,
With every gust, they ask for more!

Secrets Beneath the Boughs

In shadows deep, gossip flows free,
From acorns to bees, who's next to see?
The grass whispers secrets so absurd,
Of dancing toads and a jealous bird.

Twirling in mud, frogs join the fun,
While rabbits race, pretending to run.
Each leafy stage holds a funny show,
As nature's talents steal the glow!

Autumn's Gentle Murmur

The leaves chuckle, dressed in gold,
As pumpkins plot, or so I'm told.
They roll and bounce, with glee anew,
In this silly season, oh what a view!

The cider spills, the laughter's loud,
While corn stalks sway, like a wild crowd.
With every gust, the giggles fly,
Autumn's gags, oh my, oh my!

Choreography of Nature's Breath

In the breeze, the leaves do twirl,
As squirrels dodge in a frantic whirl.
Branches giggle, a comical sight,
While mushrooms burst into sporadic delight.

Breezy ballet, the dance goes on,
Tickling noses, then quickly gone.
Acorns ambush with a plop and a pop,
Nature's giggles, it never will stop.

Whispers of Autumn

A leaf slips, a slippery trip,
It tumbles down with a cheeky zip.
Crickets chirp in wise-guy hoots,
While owls snicker in beaky suits.

Raccoons rummage, oh what a fuss,
Those sneaky bands of masked excess.
Coughing up crumbs with every bite,
Their fallback plan? Just blame the night.

Reflections in the Canopy

Sunbeams filter, a silly show,
Leaves play peek-a-boo, just like so!
Pigeons strut in their funny flair,
While shadows dance in the crisp cool air.

Clouds above make faces in white,
Declaring the sky a comical sight.
A gust sends a dandelion fluff,
As laughter echoes, it's never enough!

Dance of Fallen Petals

Petals popcorn from boughs so grand,
As bees bumbling, join the band.
With each plop, a giggling ground,
Nature's joke all around is found.

Blades of grass wave in giggly glee,
Like quips exchanged at a comedy spree.
Butterflies flit with a winking toast,
In this leafy circus, we laugh the most.

Nature's Soft Resonation

Whispers of wind with a giggling touch,
A squirrel quips, 'I've eaten too much!'
Branches chuckle, bending low,
While flowers laugh at the world below.

Butterflies tease with their flitting show,
Chasing each other, 'You won't catch me, though!'
The brook bubbles with a giddy trill,
Nature's laughter flows, a joyful thrill.

Dancing in the Dappled Light

Sunbeams play in a playful chase,
While shadows dance at a blushing pace.
Leaves can't help but rustle with glee,
'Who can twirl best? Come dance with me!'

Frogs leap high, then take a bow,
"Can you leap like us? Show us how!"
Daisies sway, all dressed in white,
As they giggle in the dappled light.

Reverberations of Woodland Dreams

In the thicket, a bear tells a joke,
With such a punchline, the trees nearly choke!
The owls roll their eyes, "Not this again!"
The squirrels snicker, 'Let's hear it, friend!'

Breezes tease with a tickling hand,
Rustling secrets across the land.
Mice hold a council, debating with flair,
On who's the silliest creature out there.

Melodies of Mottled Ground

The path is alive with a jolly sound,
As pebbles jive on the mottled ground.
Crickets chirp in a raucous tune,
While rabbits dance under the watchful moon.

The mushrooms giggle, "Join us, friends!"
As twinkling fireflies show their trends.
With each step taken, laughter thrives,
Nature's symphony is alive with jives.

Intricate Patterns of Fluttering Dreams

In the park, a squirrel prances,
Chasing shadows, making glances.
A leaf shimmies down with grace,
To land smack on a dog's face.

Twirling round in sunny rays,
Dancing leaves, in playful ways.
They whisper secrets as they play,
Winging dreams like birds in May.

A child giggles, runs about,
Trying to shoo the leaves, no doubt.
But they tickle her nose instead,
Leaving her in giggles, red.

So here we laugh, in leaf-filled cheer,
As nature's jesters gather near.
With every flutter, silly schemes,
We smile at life and fluttering dreams.

Dialogue of Shadows and Light

Two leaves bicker on a tree,
One shouts loud, "Come chat with me!"
The sun beams down, a bright delight,
Whispers, "Why argue, when it's bright?"

Shadows stretch, and giggles sound,
As leaves tumble softly to the ground.
"I'm lighter, funnier," one leaf brags,
While the other dons a crown of rags.

A breeze joins in, just for fun,
Tickling words, the warmth of sun.
They argue back, but all in jest,
Just two leaves needing a rest.

In the end, the laughter flows,
As colors swirl and playful glows.
In whimsy's dance, they take their flight,
In a dialogue of shadows and light.

Embrace of the Bipartisan Season

Two trees debate, with leaves in hand,
One shouts, "We're a united band!"
The other rolls its leafy eyes,
"Don't you see the humor in our ties?"

Colors clash in vibrant hues,
While critters giggle at the view.
"One side's red, and one is gold!"
They tease, as autumn's chill takes hold.

Fallen leaves in piles so deep,
Squirrels hop and freely leap.
They argue still, as branches sway,
"Who made you king?" "I'm here to stay!"

Yet in this playful, leafy fight,
They dance together, oh what a sight!
In this embrace of differing cheer,
Hilarity reigns in the atmosphere.

Reverberations of Dappled Paths

On pathways where the sunlight sighs,
Leaves skip past, under azure skies.
One whispers, "Shall we mix it up?"
While another calls out, "I'll take a cup!"

Puddles laugh with every drip,
As leaves miss the road and do a flip.
Bouncing here and bouncing there,
A symphony of laughter fills the air.

A dog chases with joyous glee,
While birds enjoy the melody.
"Catch me if you can!" the leaves dare,
But end up tangled in a nearby hair.

With every rustle, a funny tale,
Of winds that tease, and joking gales.
The paths they take are full of fun,
In a world of light beneath the sun.

The Language of Leaffall

Nature's whispers in a rustle,
Trees gossiping all their hustle.
Squirrels chime in with a wiggle,
As branches play tag and giggle.

A leaf does a pirouette with flair,
Twisting mid-air, without a care.
The ground looks up, meets a face,
And starts to laugh at the leaf's wild race.

A conifer shouts, 'Pine is divine!'
While oaks declare, 'No, I'm the spine!'
Maples boast hues, brightly in show,
As everyone joins in the leafflow.

But the path is littered with chatter,
And who knew wind was such a scatter?
In this dance of colors every fall,
Chaos! Oh my, nature's a ball!

Echoing Through the Timberlands

In the forest, a woodpecker knocks,
Bouncing sounds like loud tick-tocks.
A beaver joins with a splashy beat,
Creating rhythms, oh, what a treat!

Leaves tumble down with a playful hop,
Each one a comic, ready to drop.
They land with a plop and say, 'Hello!',
In a chorus of colors, a grand show!

A rabbit hears, and leaps with grace,
Furry legs in a merry race.
They giggle, they wiggle, through the glade,
As the trees laugh loudly, their jokes never fade.

A murmuring brook adds in a dash,
With gurgles and bubbles, what a splash!
Together they conjure a woodland jest,
As timberlands thrive in a lively quest!

A Tapestry of Colors Unfurled

In the woods where colors blend,
Fallen leaves boast of trends,
A red one struts, 'I'm all the rage!'
While brown shrugs, 'I'll go with age!'

A golden leaf shimmies side to side,
Saying, 'Come dance; it's a silly ride!'
While whispers of green giggle along,
Singing tunes of nature's song.

Branches weave tales as they sway,
'Watch the leaves!' they laugh and say.
'I'm stuck in this breeze like a kite,
While you all play, I just might!'

The air is thick with jokes and cheer,
As even the bark joins in with a sneer.
This tapestry of colors in flight,
Fills the forest with laughter and light!

Transient Songs of Woods

The trees hum tunes of yesteryear,
With leaves that sway and disappear.
A hickory sings, 'Join me for fun!'
While oaks just roll their eyes, 'Not done!'

In this concert of chirps and pops,
Nature's symphony never stops.
A thrush throws in a cheeky riff,
The woodlands dance; what a gift!

The orange leaf hiccups mid-flight,
Waving goodbye in the sunlight.
Branches play air guitar with flair,
As nature's laughter fills the air.

Who knew that woods could be so silly?
With all this fun, it's never chilly!
In these transient songs, one can glean,
Nature as a jester, ever serene!

A Covey of Listenings

In the forest, whispers fly,
Squirrels gossip with a sigh.
Every rustle, every squeak,
Makes the branches seem to speak.

A rabbit hops, then stops to stare,
Wonders where the breeze might fare.
The jokes of trees are rather tall,
They chuckle softly, one and all.

Leaves conspire to tell a tale,
Of wind that trips and starts to sail.
A dance of shadows plays on ground,
While acorns drop without a sound.

Birds snicker from their leafy seats,
As nature shares her funny feats.
If only we could hear them clear,
The punchlines whispered right in ear.

Layers of Emotion in the Undergrowth

Underneath where shadows blend,
A patch of laughter seems to send.
Mice share secrets, piquant glee,
While beetles march in symmetry.

With every crunch beneath our feet,
Crickets giggle, oh so sweet.
Vines tease one another tight,
Swinging low with all their might.

An autumn breeze begins to blow,
Disguised as mischief, oh so slow.
Each leaf rolls by like silly hats,
Playing pranks on cheerful cats.

The ground is alive with mirth and cheer,
Nature's laughter ringing clear.
In this colorful joke parade,
Every shade finds a way to fade.

The Softest Footfalls of Fall

In crisp air, footfalls softly crawl,
Every step begins to call.
A squirrel's tail flicks with delight,
As leaves take flight in quick twilight.

Waltzing leaves perform their show,
Like ballet stars that spin and flow.
Giggles catch on branches high,
As pumpkins wink and lonely sigh.

A frolicsome wind starts to play,
Tossing hats from heads away.
While mischief hides beneath the rocks,
Laughter tumbles like ticking clocks.

Underfoot, the world is jest,
Soft crunches sing of nature's fest.
As sunset glows and shadows meet,
Each falling leaf brings jokes so sweet.

Grasping the Moment Through Decay

In the drapery of dusk's embrace,
Leaves scatter with unhurried grace.
A gaggle of geese honks in the air,
Each honk a prank, a light-hearted dare.

Dancing down from branches tall,
Golden treasures begin to fall.
With each soft thud, they tease and play,
In the rustling world where giggles stay.

Pine cones drop like tiny bombs,
Creating cracks, a jest that charms.
As crickets chirp their varied tunes,
A symphony of giggles blooms.

Even as time takes its toll,
Nature knows just how to console.
In the cycle where laughter stays,
We find delight in faded rays.

Unspoken Stories of the Grove

In the grove, whispers sneak,
Squirrels debate, while owls peek.
Branches giggle, trees crack a smile,
As winds play hide and seek for a while.

Nutty gossip floats in the air,
Leaves giggle while swirling in flair.
Bugs in bow ties, dancing with ease,
All join in for the grand tree tease.

Beneath the shade, laughter takes flight,
As shadows dance in morning light.
Chipmunks doing the charleston right,
While the sun dips low, ending the night.

In leafy suits, the crowd feels grand,
Nature's humor, a humorous band.
With every rustle, a joke unfolds,
In this woodland, joy never gets old.

A Symphony of Rustling Colors

Leaves rustle soft like ticklish feet,
Nature's orchestra can't be beat.
Frogs croak tunes from the muddy banks,
While crickets chirp with little pranks.

Golden yellows and reds compete,
A leafy show that can't be discreet.
A butterfly trips, falls in delight,
As petals giggle in pure twilight.

Acorns drop with a comic sound,
Mice scamper by, all around.
Branches jive, swaying with flair,
Making laughter dance in the air.

The sunset blushes, nature's own muse,
Crafting colors that never lose.
A canvas painted with giggling hues,
Isn't it funny how joy imbues!

Voices from the Understory

In the underbrush, secrets confide,
Where grasshoppers hop and bumblebees glide.
Mushrooms chuckle, wearing their caps,
As rabbits gossip in cozy gaps.

With every rustle, a joke was born,
From dawn till dusk, all are sworn.
The ferns dance like they can't stay still,
As the sun tickles, with a playful thrill.

Worms write poems in squiggly lines,
While lizards lounge sipping sunshine wines.
Little creatures in a grand review,
Sharing punchlines beneath skies so blue.

Nature's wit in a leafy embrace,
Got trees grinning in their leafy lace.
In the understory, life feels right,
With laughter echoing through the night.

Tapestry of Timeless Trees

Old trees whisper tales of yore,
With branches stretching, never a bore.
One tells of a bear who tried to fly,
While the others chuckle and roll an eye.

A squirrel's quest for a nut gone wrong,
Is sung in the wind, a comical song.
Roots wiggle like they're in a dance,
While the breeze joins in, taking a chance.

Beneath the bark, jesters hide well,
With acorn hats and a nutty spell.
Their laughter ripples through leaves and twigs,
Crafting enchantment with nature's jigs.

In this tapestry, all are bound,
With funny stories that resound.
A forest of humor, rich and free,
Nature's jokes live eternally.

The Fragility of the Transient

A breeze tickles branches, oh what a tease,
Leaves dance like clowns, swaying with ease.
One's jolly tumble makes another pout,
In this leafy circus, there's laughter about.

When the wind sneezes, they scatter away,
Like confetti on birthdays, in a foolish display.
Their short-lived joke makes the crow chuckle,
As trees roll their eyes at this leafy shuffle.

But soon they'll return, with tales to regale,
Of prancing around in a glorious gale.
Though fragile and fleeting, their humor's divine,
In nature's grand dance, they truly do shine.

Whispers of Nostalgia

Remember the days when the wind would howl?
Leaves flipped and flopped as if in a prowl.
Each rustling giggle, a tickle of time,
Recalls our own childhood, oh how sublime!

With every gust, trickster whispers tease,
"Hey you there! Catch us, if you please!"
The ground now littered with memories bright,
Leaves plotting their antics under moonlight.

As seasons parade, they dress up for laughs,
In gowns of gold, they play leafy crafts.
With a wink and a nod, they drift like a sigh,
Those whispers of yore make the heart fly high.

Memoirs of a Rustling Whisper

In the forest of giggles, where secrets convene,
A shy leaf quivers, it's hardly serene.
With tales of a squirrel that danced on a whim,
It shuffles and chuckles, almost a hymn.

A leaf's recollection of yesterday's prank,
When an acorn fell, and the whole tree shrank.
With a chuckle it shares how it wobbled and swayed,
Giggling softly, as memories replayed.

Though the bark may grow older, those tales never fade,
Laughter etches stories, in sunshine and shade.
Each flutter and flutter of this vibrant parade,
Is proof that life's best when shared and conveyed.

Balance in the Breath of Nature

A leaf hiccups loudly, as it sways from the tree,
"Catch me if you can!", it shouts with glee.
Some other leaves giggle, arms stretched in flight,
"Stop stealing the show! We'll join in tonight!"

The branches hold secrets of a playful band,
While twigs play tuba with a woodpecker's hand.
With laughter and rustles, the air starts to spin,
As every green actor joins in with a grin.

The balance is off, as they tumble and jive,
Like a dance party blooming, oh how they thrive!
In the breath of the wild, with whispers of cheer,
Life's a comical show, with nature's veneer.

Shadows of Silvered Green

In a sunlit glade, the squirrels play,
Chasing shadows that dance and sway.
One trips on a root, gives a shout,
Leaves giggle softly as he pouts.

A butterfly laughs, flutters with glee,
While a wise old owl rolls eyes, you see.
"Watch where you leap!" it hoots in jest,
But the squirrel just sighs, feeling oppressed.

A ladybug joins with a tiny cheer,
"Don't worry, friend, we're all pioneers!"
Together they frolic, nimbly around,
In the switchback whispers of the ground.

As twilight falls, shadows stretch long,
The forest hums its evening song.
With laughter aloft, they scamper away,
Under a sky where the fireflies play.

Conversations with the Breeze

The wind comes whistling, a cheeky sprite,
"Did you hear the one about the kite?"
"No," chirps a robin, puffed up with pride,
"I bet it flew high, with the clouds as its guide!"

"Not quite!" giggles wind with a twist,
"It got tangled in thorns, oh what a tryst!
It cried, 'Help me, help!' to the leafless trees,
But they chuckled and said, 'We're not here to tease!'

A nearby gust, with a hearty laugh,
Joined in the jest, "What a curious path!
I've seen fish dance, and cats that skateboard,
On this wild adventure, there's never a bore!"

So up in the branches, where secrets are spun,
The breeze winks brightly, the laughter's begun.
Whirling and swaying, it shares every tale,
Of unspoken friendships, where laughter prevails.

Cradled by the Forest

In a green nook where the ferns sprawl wide,
A family of ants takes a grand, silly ride.
"Hold on tight!" one shouts, but they tumble with flair,
As acorns roll over, without a care!

A chipmunk watches, jaws stuffed with a prize,
Unable to stop the laughter that flies.
"Is this a circus? A comedy show?"
He giggles so much, he drops his nut low!

A raccoon wanders by, slapping his knee,
"It's the funniest thing that I ever did see!
These tiny nutters are wild and free,
What a ruckus they make; they should charge a fee!"

As dusk drapes the trees in shadows so deep,
The forest joins in, with giggles to keep.
Nestled in laughter, where memories bloom,
Together they play, in the twilight's soft gloom.

The Language of Falling Flora

Leaves flutter about like they're in a race,
Trying to outshine the next in their place.
One shouts, "I'm first!" as it spins gently down,
While the others just giggle, "You'll fall with a frown!"

A wise old maple, with branches so wide,
Chimes in with a chuckle, "Let's take this in stride.
Falling's an art, not a stumble or flop!
Join in the fun, let's not make it stop!"

With a rustle and tussle, they sway in delight,
A confetti parade on a breezy night.
"Next to me, leaf, come take a seat,
We'll bounce through the air, this dance is a treat!"

So in swirling circles, they glimmer and fall,
A grand spectacle, enchanting us all.
Nature's own laughter, on this crisp autumn day,
In a whimsical waltz, they drift far away.

Rustling Chronicles

In the park, leaves play tag,
Whispering secrets with each wag.
Squirrels chase while branches sway,
Nature's laughter starts the day.

A gust arrives, leaves take flight,
Dancing off in pure delight.
Caught in a swirl, they twirl around,
Nature's pranksters can astound!

Fallen bits become a throne,
For mice who dance, all on their own.
In every rustle, a tale unfolds,
Of summer fun and autumn's gold.

With every crunch, they giggle loud,
Joining the lighthearted crowd.
Through the branches, a soft tease,
Nature's joy floats on the breeze.

Memories Carried on the Breeze

Leaves gossip softly in a line,
Recalling days so sweet and fine.
A chilled wind takes them for a spin,
Plotting mischief where they've been.

Once friends with twigs, now on their way,
Sharing tales of yesterday.
With each rustle, laughter rings,
A comedy to unclad springs.

Bouncing off a picnic spread,
Stealing crumbs, then off they fled.
If leaves could giggle, oh, what cheer,
Their jokes clear, crisp, and sincere.

Through the trees, they break the norm,
Breezy jesters, weather warm.
As they flutter, the memories please,
Funny tales in rustling trees.

Ode to the Shimmering Foliage

Oh, shiny leaves with green attire,
Wobbling 'round like they're on fire.
As sunlight kisses, they start to gleam,
A leafy cabaret, bursting with dream!

They quip and jest, a leafy crew,
With fluttering skirts in emerald hue.
One rogue leaf shimmies, takes a dive,
Only to land with a happy jive!

In the autumn, they have a ruckus,
Some play hopscotch, what a circus!
Spinning round with flair so bold,
Fabulous tales of joy they hold.

With the breeze, they surely cackle,
Their giggles unfold with every crackle.
From tree to ground, they leap with glee,
Nature's carol, wild and free.

Resonance of Time's Passage

Once green sprites in sunny glow,
Now golden crunches under toe.
Leaves discuss the seasons' change,
Telling tales and feeling strange.

Years might pass, but they remain,
Echoes bouncing through the rain.
In every swivel, each little spin,
A journey shared, where laughs begin.

From childhood parks to weddings bright,
Leaves witness love beneath moonlight.
Heartfelt whispers, as time flows,
Smirking at how fast it goes.

In the wind, old memories hoot,
Leaves chuckle soft in their pursuit.
Funny how they join the race,
Fleeting time, yet we're in place.

The Murmurs of Memory-Laden Branches

In the breeze, whispers play,
Telling jokes of yesterday,
Branches chuckle, leaves so sly,
As squirrels plot, 'Oh my, oh my!'

Gossip flows from twig to root,
Winking at a passing brute,
'Who knew acorns could be fun?'
They giggle 'til the day is done.

Rusty tales from summer's past,
Acorns falling, what a blast!
'Last year's nuts were quite a sight,'
One leaf cackled, laughing light.

With each rustle, mischief sings,
As playful winds glide on their wings,
Branches sway with jokes so fine,
Creating memes, both leaf and pine!

Fluttering Secrets in the Twilight

Secrets dance on dusky air,
Beneath the trees, stories flare,
One leaf whispers, 'Watch the show!'
As shadows stretch, they steal the glow.

Who's the biggest? Who's the best?
Critters argue, they jest, they jest!
A brave old tree rolls back its bark,
And claims its youth was quite a lark.

Laughter echoes through the night,
Fluttering leaves take to flight,
'Remember when we were so spry?'
They quip and chirp, laughing high.

The wind joins in, a jester proud,
Tickling branches, drawing a crowd,
As twilight fades, their voices blend,
The fun of leaves will never end!

Rustle and Rapture

In the rustle, there's delight,
A leafy choir sings tonight,
One goes 'Shhh!' while others laugh,
As they plot their leafy math.

'True or false, how many passed?'
A leaf confesses, 'I fell fast!'
They count the falls, the laughs accrue,
'Next time, I won't be so blue.'

A windy giggle stirs the trees,
Leaves agree with subtle ease,
'We're quite the troupe, delightful mess,'
They hum in joyous leafiness.

With each sway comes laughter's ring,
Nature's stage hosts a wild fling,
Whispers weave through every bough,
The joke of life is right here, now!

The Sound of Leaves at Dusk

As dusk falls, the leaves convene,
Hatching plans quite unforeseen,
'Who can sway the hardest here?'
A giggle bursts, oh dear, oh dear!

'It's a party, come one, come all!'
The leaves rally, heed the call,
And off they go, a rustling band,
With every swing, they make their stand.

Twilight brings a playful glow,
'Tell your tales, and off we go!'
One leaf spun a dizzy spin,
While others cheered, let the games begin!

They rattle on through darkening skies,
With jokes that bridge the world's goodbyes,
'Crack a smile, shine bright like us,'
The trees agree, in verdant trust!

Visions of Verdant Soliloquies

In the grove, the branches sway,
Whispering secrets, come what may.
A squirrel giggles at my shoes,
I trip and land in morning dew.

The leaves gossip with the breeze,
Sharing tales of wild misdeeds.
A rabbit chuckles in the sun,
While I ponder my next big run.

Bright petals dance with silly flair,
As I attempt a charming stare.
But nature's humor strikes me low,
With pollen tickles, watch me go!

Oh, the pranks that nature plays,
In her leafy, green arrays.
I laugh and snort, a joyful sound,
As dandelions spin around.

Tender Regrets of the Silk Road

A merchant's hat flew off his head,
Chased by thoughts of soft, warm bread.
He stumbled on a patch of grass,
And laughed as he fell down, alas!

Silks draped low, then caught a breeze,
Dancing 'round like playful tease.
Camels winked with knowing smiles,
As cloth and dust went 'cross the miles.

My basket's filled with fruits of fall,
Yet figs now sit upon the wall.
"Which way to go?" I loudly quiz,
While squirrels plot their next whiz fizz!

Oh, the tales from that dusty way,
Pack your snacks and come out to play.
The road is long, the humor sweet,
Come nibble on these jokester treats!

Harmony in a Symphony of Greens

In a forest where mischief thrives,
The reeds play tunes that make us jive.
A frog on a leaf sings off-key,
While ants march forth, in harmony!

Branches shimmy, trunks do sway,
As critters dance the day away.
The rhythm flows, a leafy fun,
While shadows tease beneath the sun.

A chorus of giggles fills the air,
As trees perform with style and flair.
Yet, in this show, I trip and fall,
And no one hears that silly call.

Laughter echoes, without a doubt,
In this wild green, there's no room for pout.
Join the revels, don't be shy,
In nature's jest, we all comply!

A Solstice of Silence

A breeze whispers with playful cheer,
Leaves chuckle softly, can you hear?
Sunbeams tickle the forest ground,
Where merry critters bounce around.

The shadows stretch in silly ways,
As time wobbles through summer days.
A turtle grins, oh what a sight,
While crickets serenade the night.

In the quiet, laughter prances,
While sudden gusts ignite some chances.
A solo dance, a leaf takes flight,
Twirling, twirling, 'til it's night.

Nature's pause reveals the jest,
The ultimate, calming quest.
In silence, joy can grow so loud,
We all join in, a happy crowd.

Serene Whispers in Twilight

In the evening glow, the branches dance,
As squirrels gossip in their leafy pants.
Each rustle hints at secrets shared,
While nearby, a cat just unprepared.

A breeze plays tricks on the grass so spry,
Tickling toes as it flutters by.
A giggle from the willows rolls,
And laughter fills the air in trolls.

Roots of Memory

Forgotten snacks in the garden bed,
Cucumber peels where raccoons tread.
Each footfall stirs the tales long past,
Of cheeky critters that dart so fast.

The ancient oak with its knobby knees,
Whispers tales like an old grandee.
"Remember when we stole the pies?"
Oh, what fun to hear the sighs!

The Archive of Arborvitae

Beneath the boughs, a meeting occurs,
A debate on acorns and childish furs.
Squirrels convene with their thimble hats,
While birds exchange glances like little spats.

Each branch serves as a dusty tome,
Recording all mischiefs that roam.
With branches waving, they muse aloud,
"Who's the funniest in this leafy crowd?"

Fleeting Shadows Under the Oaks

There's a shadow dance, a game of tease,
As critters prance with the greatest of ease.
The dappled sun beams down so bright,
While a snail takes its time, what a sight!

From cozy nests, the gossip flows,
"Did you hear about the bush that grows?"
Witty whispers take to the air,
As a dung beetle joins in with flair.

Interludes in Between the Trees

A squirrel danced in bright green spats,
While owls laughed at his acrobatic flats.
The pine trees giggled with glee above,
As gossip flew like a fluttering dove.

A raccoon stole snacks on a moonlit spree,
But the rabbits called, 'Hey, that's meant for tea!'
They gossip and laugh, their noses twitching,
While the breeze whispers back, always glitching.

The bees made a buzz, all choir-like hymns,
While flowers swayed, doing their whimsical whims.
A clever fox sang, 'What's the latest craze?'
The forest cheerfully joined in the praise.

And who could forget the owl's loud hoot?
With tales of drama in feathered pursuit.
Nature's stage, hosting a comic show,
With laughter and mischief, put on a glow.

Echoes of Turquoise Twilight

A butterfly flapped, wearing shades of blue,
While the brooks sang, 'We're cooler than you!'
The mushrooms giggled, their hats all a-twitch,
As fireflies danced, sparking up a glitch.

The sun took a dip in a turquoise hue,
While crickets chirped, 'What's new, what's new?'
The stars threw a party, all twinkled in time,
Swaying with laughter, not caring for rhyme.

A wily raccoon wore a mask of delight,
While the owls hooted, "Oh, what a sight!"
The wind whispered softly, jokes up it spun,
As dusk painted laughter and merged all in one.

The trees told secrets, wrapped in their tales,
Spinning yarns of knaves navigating gales.
In twilight's embrace, they all mixed and swirled,
A whimsy-filled night in a magical world.

Tales Carried by the Seasonal Wind

A leaf took flight on a breeze swift and sly,
Shouting, 'Catch me if you can!' with a sigh.
The wind blew a laugh, quite merry and free,
While squirrels rolled over, munching their brie.

The daisies were bold, cracking jokes by the path,
While the hedgehogs scuttled, avoiding the wrath.
The autumn played tricks, painting all reds,
As pumpkins looked round, sporting green heads!

Little acorns tumbled, landing with cheers,
Giving high-fives as they conquered their fears.
A wise old oak chuckled, 'Life's one big dance!'
With a twist and a twirl, they took every chance.

The wind carried giggles through every branch,
Tickling the leaves in a whimsical dance.
In nature's embrace, they found their delight,
And spun tales of joy, throughout day and night.

Nature's Gentle Confessions

The brook babbles secrets, with a splash and a wink,
As the frogs croaked out laughter, refusing to think.
A playful breeze tickles the flowers' soft cheeks,
While butterflies gossip of love that peaks.

A sneaky little mouse wrote jokes on a leaf,
Sharing them round, spreading comic relief.
The sun winked down, a golden cheerleader,
As the clouds inflated, becoming a theater.

The owls held a meeting, debating who's wise,
While the bats swung in, donning friendship ties.
The night glowed with laughter, a comedy scene,
As the moon pulled a prank, making shadows obscene.

In every eavesdropping rustle, there's glee,
Nature's own laughter as vast as the sea.
With every flutter, giggle, and sigh,
Whimsy unravels in the midnight sky.

Murmurs Beneath the Boughs

Rustling whispers share silly tales,
Of squirrels stuck in their acorn trails.
The branches chuckle, swaying like pros,
While owls pretend they know all the woes.

A chipmunk trips on its tiny feet,
Joking that it can't handle the heat.
Leaves burst into laughter, swaying around,
As the wind giggles, creating a sound.

The raccoon dances without a care,
Claiming he invented that trendy flair.
Beneath the boughs, in a comical sight,
Nature's court jesters frolic in delight.

Oh, tangled in branches, they swing and roll,
Their laughter echoing, a jolly patrol.
Each rustle a joke in this woodland spree,
Where even the roots join in merrily!

Secrets of the Windswept Grove

In the grove where the breezes play tricks,
The trees tell secrets with funny flicks.
A leaf fell down, but then took a bow,
Claiming it knew how to dance like a cow.

The grass tickles toes and giggles loud,
As critters gather, form a wild crowd.
A squirrel tells stories of nutty gets,
While the wind snickers, and the sun forgets.

Up in the canopy, owls are wise,
Yet they sneak peeks with mischievous eyes.
They hoot jokes about the rabbit's big ears,
As nature chuckles, drowning out fears.

With every gust, a playful spin,
The grove giggles like it's lost in a grin.
Each rustling branch a playful tease,
In this hilarious place, everyone's at ease!

Harmonies of Nature's Canvas

In the meadow, a hare finds a beat,
Bouncing along on its nimble feet.
With a twist and a turn, it leads the dance,
While the daisies shake in a laugh-filled trance.

Birds chirp in chorus, each note a jest,
Mimicking owls in their Sunday best.
While butterflies flutter, stealing the show,
As the sun winkles at every row.

A busy ant thinks it's quite the star,
Critiquing the flowers from afar.
They giggle at clouds, so fluffy and bold,
Whispering secrets that never get old.

Nature's palette a whimsical tune,
As the moon giggles with the stars in June.
The canvas of life, a riot of cheer,
Leaves rejoicing, with nothing to fear.

Shadows on the Forest Floor

Silly shadows dance upon the ground,
While the moonlight twirls to a giggly sound.
Mice play tag with the whispering winds,
Teasing the fox as the laughter begins.

The trees play peekaboo with every sway,
Trying to catch the sunlight at play.
Roots tell stories of their underground trips,
While everyone's laughing at the acorn slips.

A cat sits lazy, watching the fun,
Rolling its eyes at the dog on the run.
Tails wagging wildly, it jests with glee,
Chasing the whispers, as free as can be.

Through rustles and chuckles, the night never ends,
In this funny forest, where laughter transcends.
Each shadow a joke, every breeze a jest,
Where the heart of the woods feels truly blessed.

Diary of a Wandering Leaf

In the breeze, I take my flight,
Catching laughs under sunlight.
I tickle branches, play a jest,
Floating off, I'm quite the pest.

I danced with flowers, bold and bright,
Whispered secrets, took my height.
A squirrel thought me quite a prize,
But all I wanted were blue skies.

I pranked a frog, he hopped around,
My giggles echoed off the ground.
A spider spun a websling net,
I flitted through, it wasn't set.

With each gust, I make my way,
Through crowded trees, I laugh and sway.
A life of fun, I won't deny,
Just a leaf that loves to fly.

Symphony of the Season's Change

A trumpet blast from autumn's horn,
With every rustle, new tales born.
The wind conducts a leaf ballet,
As colors dance and spin away.

One leaf wore red, another gold,
Each tried to break the winter's cold.
Yet snowy flakes would steal the show,
A messy night of leaf and snow!

The pine trees groaned, 'This is absurd!'
While acorns laughed without a word.
The branches swayed, with vibe so loose,
In nature's band, there's no excuse.

With every shift, the seasons bicker,
While I spin 'round like a goofy sticker.
The concert flows, I join the rhyme,
A leaf in sync with playful time.

Tales Written in Chlorophyll

In a storybook of vibrant green,
I scribble tales of what I've seen.
A leaf's life filled with silly laughs,
Like running races with the grass.

There's drama too, with wind so bold,
Blustering tales of leaves gone cold.
I met a twig that claimed to fly,
But only managed to look shy.

A beetle blushed when I went near,
As I tickled him, he shed a tear.
We laughed aloud, what a delight,
Two pals at play, oh what a sight!

From chlorophyll, my stories weave,
In hues of joy, I shall believe.
With each new page, I spread my cheer,
A leaf's funny tale, forever clear.

Swaying in Silent Conversations

Beneath the boughs, I sway and peek,
Whispers share the secrets we seek.
A breeze can tell a joke or two,
As branches giggle, they like to woo.

A fluffy cloud floats by with grace,
I ask it for a little space.
It rolled its eyes in pure delight,
And offered rain, a silly fight!

And when the sun pretends to hide,
I poke my friends from side to side.
The shadows play, a game we start,
Invisible, yet close at heart.

In rustled tones, we weave our tale,
Of windy days, we will not fail.
As laugh lines etch on bark and leaf,
In silent chats, we find our relief.

A Brush with the Past in the Present

Once I found a leaf so grand,
It whispered tales from a distant land.
I laughed as it danced in the breeze,
Sharing secrets with the trees.

But chill winds blew; it got a fright,
And tumbled down in sheer delight.
I chased it round, we made a scene,
A leaf and me, a comical dream.

Each day it rolls with a joyful cheer,
Wearing dust like a crown, sincere.
I often trip, oh what a sight!
With nature's jester, I take flight.

So here's to leaves with funny quirks,
In their rustling fun, the world perks.
They teach us to laugh, to sway and spin,
In the dance of life, we all can win.

The Ballet of Decaying Life

In autumn's glow, a ballet begins,
Leaves twirl down with mischievous grins.
They leap and spin, in a waltz of decay,
Every flutter a joke, come join the play!

One slipped from the branch with a graceful shout,
"Catch me if you can!" it spun about.
I stumbled and fumbled, leaf on my head,
A crown of embarrassment, oh, what a spread!

They pile on the ground, a colorful bed,
With crunching sounds, the laughter spread.
And squirrels show off in a lively jive,
In this quirky dance, we feel so alive!

So when you see leaves make their descent,
Join in the laughter, it's time well spent.
For life's a ballet, so silly and bright,
With nature's humor, we take to flight.

In the Thicket of Lost Words

There's a thicket where whispers reside,
Words dance with leaves, all side by side.
One leaf said, "I'm a dictionary, look!"
While another just rolled away with a book!

They exchange their stories, crisp and neat,
"I'm rusty with riddles!" said one with a tweet.
As they chuckle and cackle, a mystery forms,
In their playful chaos, everything conforms.

I wandered in, lost in their talk,
"Did you hear that joke about the old oak?"
They burst into laughter, spit out a pun,
"Tree-mendous humor, we're never done!"

So if you find words in the leaves that sway,
Join in their banter, don't shy away!
In the thicket of laughter, wisdom unfurls,
With silly old leaves, let's spin in twirls.

Unseen Threads of Connection

Leaves weave a tapestry, hidden and bright,
Every flutter connects us, just out of sight.
I waved to a leaf from my cozy chair,
It winked back at me, with a playful air!

One leaf yelled, "Hey, I'm a fabric of tales!"
I answered, "Got threads that mimic gales?"
Together we laughed at the world's crazy spins,
These unseen threads make us all kin.

With every gust, a giggling affair,
They twist and shout like they just don't care.
"Let's stitch a quilt of joy in the park!"
They fly by, leaving laughter like sparks.

In this patchwork of nature, strangers unite,
With humorous winds, our souls take flight.
So toss in your jokes, let your laughter flow,
In the threads we find, together we grow!

Breath of the Wild Symphony

In the forest, a rustle, a sound,
A squirrel on a mission, round and round.
Leaves chatter gossip, branches shake hands,
While nature's orchestra plays in strange bands.

A butterfly winks, says, "Look at me!"
A flower responds, "I'm your VIP."
The sun beams down with a grin so wide,
While the river dances, a playful tide.

The grass has jokes, tickling toes,
While rocks wear hats, or so it goes.
In this wild cacophony of glee,
Who knew nature's comedy could be so free?

So laugh with the leaves, they know the trick,
In their leafy jokes, find humor quick.
With every gust and flutter, you'll see,
The forest giggles, inviting thee!

The Language of Unfurling

A bud bursts forth, with a pop and a cheer,
Whispers of petals, 'Spring has found us here!'
In the breeze, a leaf does a jig,
While a worm rolls by, thinking it's big.

The wind tells tales of the clouds up high,
As clovers giggle, 'Watch out, we might fly!'
Dandelions puff out their fuzzy heads,
While ants march on, declaring their threads.

A sunflower winks at a passing bee,
Saying, 'I'm the star of our floral spree.'
The grass tickles toes, in a playful way,
And mushrooms make hats for a fancy day.

Nature speaks softly, it's language fun,
An invitation to join in the run.
With laughs and jests, let the frolic begin,
In every unfurling, joy's sure to win!

Nature's Softest Farewell

When autumn bids goodbye, it fumbles,
Leaves tumble down with giggles and grumbles.
The trees throw a party, their colors so bright,
While squirrels stuff acorns for winter's delight.

A leaf whispers, 'Don't worry, I'm fine,'
As it flutters and flips to a dance divine.
The wind plays the trumpet, shall we dance now?
The ground mutters, 'Shhh, I'm not ready, wow!'

The flowers bow low, their lesson complete,
As nature jokes back, 'Now that was sweet!'
Though cold winds might shiver and chide,
They join the laughter, where warm hearts reside.

So let's toast to change, with bags full of jest,
In nature's farewell, we're genuinely blessed.
With each soft sigh that the seasons deploy,
Nature leaves us grinning, wrapped in its joy!

The Lullaby of Decay

A crunchy leaf whispers a song so sly,
While a twig snaps back, 'Don't let it lie!'
Nature's a charmer, with a twinkle so bright,
As a sleepy old log settles down for the night.

A mushroom pops up, wearing a grin,
Says, 'Hold on tight, let the fun begin!'
With the gentle shades of twilight's blue,
The critters all gather, for a dance or two.

The breeze hums softly, a tune so sweet,
As acorns and nuts have a fancy feast.
With laughter to echo through crisp autumn air,
Even the shadows seem lighthearted and rare.

So nestle in close, as the leaves start to sway,
In the cozy embrace of a fading day.
With each fading note, let the chuckles stay,
In the lullaby sung by the world's bright decay!

The Soundtrack of Shifting Seasons

When autumn's breath begins to sing,
The squirrels dance on invisible string.
Crisp crunch, a foot in pile so grand,
Leaves plot and giggle, isn't it all planned?

Winter shivers, coats all around,
Snowflakes blushing, falling down to the ground.
Every gust is a playful tease,
As snowmen grin with frozen knees.

Spring leaps in with a sprightly chime,
Daffodils sway, it's flower prime!
Bees in suits, buzzing with glee,
Pollinating jokes beneath the tree.

Then summer smirks as the sun blares bright,
Picnics and laughter, everyone's light.
While leaves work hard to make you smile,
They crack up together for a while!

Fragments of a Breezy Ballad

In the park, the winds conspire,
Tickling noses with soft desire.
A leaf with flair does a twirl,
"Catch me if you can!" it starts to whirl!

The cloud above looks down and grins,
Watching all with silly sins.
As raindrops drip, they laugh and tease,
"Whoops! Sorry, folks, here comes a breeze!"

Each gust awakens merry tunes,
Grasshopper bands all under moons.
"Let's sing a tune of crazy dance,
While leaves go shuffling in their prance!"

In this realm where colors play,
Nature's humor brightens the day.
With whispers sweet and giggles loud,
Leaves tell tales to the merry crowd.

Call of the Woodland Spirits

In the woods, the shadows wink,
Tree trunks giggle, "Who needs a drink?"
Mossy carpets cushion the fall,
"Beware of the tickles; you'll have a ball!"

Branches call, "Come dance with me!"
"Just one twist, and let it be!"
But owls hoot, "Oh dear, oh my!
The squirrels are plotting; you can't deny!"

With whispers sweet between the trees,
Rabbits gossip about the bees.
"Why do they buzz? What's all the fuss?"
"Oh nothing," replies, "They just like to fuss!"

As moonlight spills over sleepy ground,
Leaves get tickled, and what a sound!
All the spirits, furry and slight,
Laugh together, embracing the night.

Sighs of the Whispering Woods

In the breeze, the branches sigh,
"Here comes another butterfly!"
They flutter past, a comical crew,
Making faces, as butterflies do.

The roots chuckle in earthy glee,
"Who knew we'd host a comedy spree?"
Fungus sprinkles giggles below,
"Wait 'til you see, I can do a show!"

A sudden rustle! Who's making noise?
A family of raccoons playing with toys.
"Not again," the wise old owl groans,
"Keep it down, won't you? You're shaking my bones!"

As night falls, stars doodle the sky,
Leaves whisper secrets, oh my, oh my!
In this wonderland, laughter roams free,
Where even the night gets a giggle with glee!

www.ingramcontent.com/pod-product-compliance
Lightning Source LLC
Chambersburg PA
CBHW070329120526
44590CB00017B/2841